GAWAYNE /
THE GREEN KNIGHT

A FAIRY TALE

By

CHARLTON MINER LEWIS

WITH AN INTRODUCTION
BY K. G. T. WEBSTER

First published in 1903

TO
G. R. L.

CONTENTS

GAWAIN

Fr. *Walwain* (*Brut*), *Gauvain*, *Gaugain*;
Lat. *Walganus*, *Walwanus*;
Dutch, *Walwein*, Welsh, *Gwalchmei*

Son of King Loth of Orkney, and nephew to Arthur on his mother's side, the most famous hero of Arthurian romance, The first mention of his name is in a passage of William of Malmesbury, recording the discovery of his tomb in the province of Ros in Wales. He is there described as "*Walwen qui fuit haud degener Arturis ex sorore nepos.*" Here he is said to have reigned over Galloway; and there is certainly some connexion, the character of which is now not easy to determine, between the two. In the later *Historia* of Goeffrey of Monmouth, and its French translation by Wace, Gawain plays an important and "pseudo-historic" rôle. On the receipt by Arthur of the insulting message of the Roman emperor, demanding tribute, it is he who is despatched as ambassador to the enemy's camp, where his arrogant and insulting behaviour brings about the outbreak of hostilities. On receipt of the tidings of Mordred's treachery, Gawain accompanies Arthur to England, and is slain in the battle which ensues on their landing. Wace, however, evidently knew more of Gawain than he has included in his translation.

The English Arthurian poems regard him as the type and model of chivalrous courtesy, "the fine father of nurture," and as Professor Maynadier has well remarked, "previous to the appearance of Malory's compilation it was Gawain rather than Arthur, who was the typical English hero." It is thus rather surprising to find that in the earliest preserved MSS. of

Arthurian romance, *i.e.* in the poems of Chrétien de Troyes, Gawain, though generally placed first in the list of knights, is by no means the hero par excellence. The latter part of the *Perceval* is indeed devoted to the recital of his adventures at the *Chastel Merveilleus*, but of none of Chrétien's poems is he the protagonist. The anonymous author of the *Chevalier à l'epée* indeed makes this apparent neglect of Gawain a ground of reproach against Chrétien. At the same time the majority of the short episodic poems connected with the cycle have Gawain for their hero. In the earlier form of the prose romances, *e.g.* in the *Merlin* proper, Gawain is a dominant personality, his feats rivalling in importance those ascribed to Arthur, but in the later forms such as the *Merlin* continuations, the *Tristan*, and the final *Lancelot* compilation, his character and position have undergone a complete change, he is represented as cruel, cowardly and treacherous, and of indifferent moral character. Most unfortunately our English version of the romances, Malory's *Morte Arthur*, being derived from these later forms (though his treatment of Gawain is by no means uniformly consistent), this unfavourable aspect is that under which the hero has become known to the modern reader. Tennyson, who only knew the Arthurian story through the medium of Malory, has, by exaggeration, largely contributed to this misunderstanding. Morris, in *The Defence of Guinevere*, speaks of "gloomy Gawain"; perhaps the most absurdly misleading epithet which could possibly have been applied to the "gay, gratious, and gude" knight of early English tradition.

The truth appears to be that Gawain, the Celtic and mythic origin of whose character was frankly admitted by the late M. Gaston Paris, belongs to the very earliest stage of Arthurian tradition, long antedating the crystallization of such tradition into literary form. He was certainly known in Italy at a very early date; Professor Rains has found the names of Arthur and Gawain in charters of the early 12th century, the bearers of those names being then grown to manhood; and Gawain is figured in the architrave of the north doorway of Modena cathedral, a 12th-century building. Recent discoveries have made it practically certain that there existed, prior to the extant romances, a collection of short episodic poems, devoted to the glorification of Arthur's famous nephew and his immediate kin (his brother Ghaeris, or Gareth, and his son Guinglain), the authorship of which was attributed to a Welshman, Bleheris; fragments of this collection have been preserved to us alike in the first continuation of Chrétien de Troyes *Perceval*, due to Wauchier de Densin, and in our vernacular *Gawain* poems. Among these "Bleheris" poems was one dealing with Gawain's adventures at the Grail castle, where the Grail is represented as non-Christian, and presents features strongly reminiscent of the ancient Nature mysteries. There is good ground for believing that as Grail quester and winner, Gawain preceded alike Perceval and Galahad, and that the solution of the mysterious Grail problem is to be sought rather in the tales connected with the older hero than in those devoted to the glorification of the younger knights. The explanation of the very perplexing changes which the character of Gawain has undergone appears to lie in a misunderstanding of the original sources of that character. Whether or no Gawain was a sun-hero, and he certainly possessed some of the features—we are constantly told how his strength waxed with the waxing of the sun till noontide, and then gradually decreased; he owned a steed known by a definite name le Gringalet; and a light-giving sword, Escalibur (which, as a rule, is represented as belonging to Gawain, not to Arthur)—all traits of a sun-hero—he certainly has much in common with the primitive Irish hero Cuchullin. The famous head-cutting challenge, so admirably told in *Syr Gawayne and the Grene Knighte*, was originally connected with the Irish champion. Nor was the lady of Gawain's love a mortal maiden, but the queen of the other-world. In Irish tradition the other-world is often represented as an island, inhabited by women only; and it is this "Isle of Maidens" that Gawain visits in *Diu Crone*;

9

returning therefrom dowered with the gift of eternal youth. The Chastel Merveilleus adventure, related at length by Chrétien and Wolfram is undoubtedly such an "other-world" story. It seems probable that it was this connexion which won for Gawain the title of the "Maidens' Knight," a title for which no satisfactory explanation is ever given. When the source of the name was forgotten its meaning was not unnaturally misinterpreted, and gained for Gawain the reputation of a facile morality, which was exaggerated by the pious compilers of the later Grail romances into persistent and aggravated wrong-doing; at the same time it is to be noted that Gawain is never like Tristan and Lancelot, the hero of an illicit connexion maintained under circumstances-of falsehood and treachery. Gawain, however, belonged to the pre-Christian stage of Grail tradition, and it is not surprising that writers, bent on spiritual edification, found him somewhat of a stumbling-block. Chaucer, when he spoke of Gawain coming "again out of faerie," spoke better than he knew; the home of that very gallant and courteous knight is indeed Fairy-land, and the true Gawain-tradition is informed with fairy glamour and grace.

AN EXCERPT FROM
1911 *Encyclopædia Britannica, Volume* 11

INTRODUCTION

By K. G. T. Webster

Gawain and the Green Knight is the finest representative of a great cycle of verse romances devoted wholly or principally to the adventures of Gawain. Of these there still survive in English a dozen or so; in French — the tongue in which romance most flourished — seven or eight more; and these, of course, are but a fraction of what must once have existed.

No other knight of the Round Table occupies anything like so important a place as Gawain in the literature of the middle ages. He is the first mentioned of Arthur's knights, for about 1125, ten years before Geoffrey of Monmouth dazzled the world with his revelation of King Arthur, William of Malmesbury in his *Chronicle of the Kings of England* had told of the discovery of Gawain's tomb in Ross, Wales, and had described him as Arthur's nephew and worthy second.

Where other knights quailed, Gawain was serene; where other champions were beaten, Gawain won; and where no resolution, strength, or skill could avail, Gawain succeeded by his kindness, his virtue, and his charming speech.

AN EXCERPT FROM
Sir Gawain and the Green Knight, 1917
Translated by William Allan Neilson

PREFACE

Arms and the man I sing,—not as of old
The Mantuan bard his mighty verse unrolled,
But in such humbler strains as may beseem
Light changes rung on a fantastic theme.
My tale is ancient, but the sense is new,—
Replete with monstrous fictions, yet half true;—
And, if you'll follow till the story's done,
I promise much instruction, and some fun.

CANTO I

THE GREEN KNIGHT

King Arthur and his court were blithe and gay
In high-towered Camelot, on Christmas day,
For all the Table Round were back again,
At peace with God and with their fellow-men.
Their shields hung idly on the pictured wall;
Their blood-stained banners decked the festal hall
Light footsteps, rustling on the rush-strewn floors,
And laughter, rippling down long corridors,
Attested minds at ease and hearts at play,—
Rude Mars unharnessed for love's holiday.
In the great hall the Christmas feast was done.
The level sunbeams from the setting sun
Stretched through the mullioned casements to the wall,
And wove fantastic shadows over all.
The revelry was hushed. In tranquil ease
The warriors grouped themselves by twos and threes
About the dames and damsels of the court,
And chattered careless words of small import;
But in an alcove, unobserved, apart,
Young Gawayne sat with Lady Elfinhart,
In Arthur's court no goodlier knight than he
Wore shirt of mail, or Cupid's panoply;
And Elfinhart, to Gawayne's eager eyes.

Of all heaven's treasures seemed the goodliest prize.
Now daylight faded, and the twilight gloom
Deepened the stillness in the vaulted room,
Save where upon the hearth a fitful glow
Blushed from the embers as the fire burned low.
There is a certain subtle twilight mood,
When two hearts meet in a dim solitude,
That thrills the soul e'en to the finger-tips,
And brings the heart's dear secrets to the lips.
In Gawayne's corner, as the shades grew thicker,
Four eyes waxed brighter, and two pulses quicker;
Ten minutes more of quiet talk unbroken,
And heaven alone can tell what might be spoken!
But it was not to be, for fates unequal
Compelled—but this anticipates the sequel.
Just in the nick of time, King Arthur rose
From his sedate post-prandial repose,
And called for lights. Along the shadowy aisles
His pages' footsteps pattered o'er the tiles,
Speeding to do his errand, and at once
Four tapers flickered from each silver sconce.
The scene was changed, the dreamer's dream dispelled,
And what might else have been his fate withheld
From Gawayne's grasp. So may one touch of chance
Shatter the fragile fabric of romance,
And all the heart's desire,—the joy, the trouble,—
Flash to oblivion with the bursting bubble!

But Arthur, on his kingly dais-seat,
Felt nothing of the passion and the heat
That fire young blood. He raised his warlike head
And glancing moodily around him, said:
"So have ye feasted well, my knights, this day,
And filled your hearts with revel and with play.
But to my mind that day is basely spent

16

Which passes by without accomplishment
Of some bright deed of arms or chivalry.
We rust in indolence. As well not be,
As be the minions of an idle court
Where all is gallantry and girlish sport!
Some bold adventure let our thoughts devise,
To stir our courage and to cheer our eyes."
And lo! while yet he spoke, from far away
In the thick shroud of the departed day,
Upon the frosty air of evening borne,
Came the faint challenge of a fairy horn!

King Arthur started up in mild surprise,
While knights and dames looked round with questioning eyes,
And each to other spoke some hurried word,
As, "Did you hear it?"—"What was that I heard?"
But well they knew; for you must understand
That Camelot lay close to Fairyland,
And the wild blast of fairy horns, once known,
Is straightway recognized as soon as blown,
Being a sound unique, unearthly, shrill,—
Between a screech-owl and a whip-poor-will.
The mischief is, that no one e'er can tell
Whether such heralding bodes ill or well!

The ladies of the palace looked faint fear,
Dreading some perilous adventure near;
For peril can the bravest spirits move,
When threatening not ourselves, but those we love;
But Lady Elfinhart clapped hands in glee,—
In sooth, no sentimentalist seemed she,—
And cried: "Now, brave Sir Gawayne,—O what fun!
Succor us, save us, else we are undone;
Show us the prowess of your arm this night;
I never saw a tilt by candle-light!"

Gaily she spoke, and seemed all unconcerned;
And yet a curious watcher might have learned
From a slight quaver in her laughter free
To doubt the frankness of her flippancy.
Gawayne, bewildered, looked the other way,
And wondered what she meant; for in that day
The ready wit of man was under muzzle,
And woman's heart was still an unsolved puzzle;
And Gawayne, though in valor next to none,
Wished that *her* heart had been a tenderer one.
His sword was out for any foe on earth,
And yet to face death for a lady's mirth
Seemed scarce worth while. What honor bade, he'ld do,
But would have liked to see a tear or two.

While thus he pondered, came a sudden burst
Of high-pitched fairy horn-calls, like the first,
But nearer, clearer, deadlier than before,
Blown seemingly from just outside the door.
The casements shook, the taper lights all trembled;
The bravest knight's dismay was ill-dissembled;
And as all sprang with one accord to win
Their swords and shields, stern combat to begin,
The great doors shot their bolts, and opened slowly in.

And now my laboring muse is hard beset,
For something followed such as never yet
Was writ or sung, by human voice or hand,
Save those that tell old tales from Fairyland.
"Miracles *do* not happen:"—'t is plain sense,
If you italicize the present tense;
But in those days, as rare old Chaucer tells,
All Britain was fulfilled of miracles.
So, as I said, the great doors opened wide.
In rushed a blast of winter from outside,

And with it, galloping on the empty air,
A great green giant on a great green mare
Plunged like a tempest-cleaving thunderbolt,
And struck four-footed, with an earthquake's jolt,
Plump on the hearthstone. There the uncouth wight
Sat greenly laughing at the strange affright
That paled all cheeks and opened wide all eyes;
Till after the first shock of quick surprise
The people circled round him, still in awe,
And circling stared; and this is what they saw:
Cassock and hood and hose, of plushy sheen
Like close-cut grass upon a bowling-green,
Covered his stature, from his verdant toes
To the green brows that topped his emerald nose.
His beard was glossy, like unripened corn;
His eyes shot sparklets like the polar morn.
But like in hue unto that deep-sea green
Wherewith must shine those gems of ray serene
The dark, unfathomed caves of ocean bear.
Green was his raiment, green his monstrous mare.
He rode unarmed, uncorsleted, unshielded,
Except that in his huge right hand he wielded
A frightful battle-axe, with blade as green
As coppery rust;—but the long edge shone keen.

Such was the stranger, and he turned his head
From one side to the other, and then said,
With gentle voice, most like a summer breeze
That rustles through the leaves of the green trees:
"So this is Arthur's court! My noble lord,
You said just now you felt a trifle bored,
And wished, instead of dancing, feasting, flirting,
Your gallant warriors might be exerting
Their puissance upon some worthier thing.
The wish, my lord, was worthy of a king!

It pleased me; here I am; and I intend
To serve your fancy as a faithful friend.
I bring adventure,—no hard, tedious quest,
But merely what I call a merry jest.
Let some good knight, the doughtiest of you all,
Swing this my battle-axe, and let it fall
On whatsoever part of me he will;
I will abide the blow, and hold me still;
But let him, just a twelvemonth from this day,
Come to me, if by any means he may,
And let me, if I live, pay back my best,
As he pays me. What think you of the jest?"
He said; and made a courteous bow,—the while
Lighting his features with a bright green smile;
As when June breezes, after rain-clouds pass,
Ripple in sunlight o'er the unmown grass.

The jest seemed fair indeed; but none the less
No knight showed any undue forwardness
To seize the offer. Some with laughter free
Daffed it aside; while others carelessly
Strolled to the farthest corners of the hall
As if they had not heard his words at all,
And whistled with an air of idle ease,
Or studied figures in the tapestries.
Not so Sir Gawayne. Vexed in mind he stood
With downcast eyes, and knew not what he would.
Trained in the school of chivalry to prize
His honor as the light of his dear eyes,
He held his life, his fortunes, everything,
In sacred trust for knighthood and his king,
And in the battle-field or tilting-yard
He met his foe full-fronted, and struck hard.
But now it seemed a foolish thing to throw

One's whole life to the fortune of a blow.
True valor breathes not in the braggart vaunt;
True honor takes no shame from idle taunt;
So let this wizard, if he wants to, scoff;
Why should our hero have his head cut off?

While thus Sir Gawayne, wrapped in thought intense,
Debated honor versus common sense,
The stranger knight was casting his green glance
Around the circling throng,—until by chance
He met the eyes of Lady Elfinhart,
And—did she flush?—and did the Green Knight start?
Surely a quiver twinkled in each eye;
But what of that? It need not signify:
Beneath his glance a brave man well might flush;
What wonder then that a fair maid should blush?
And as for him, no man that ever loved
Could look upon her loveliness unmoved.

Could I but picture her—ah, you would deem
My tale the figment of a poet's dream;
And if you saw her, (could such bliss be given),
You'ld think *yourself* in dreamland—or in heaven.
Not the red rapture of new-wakened roses,
When morning dew their soul of love uncloses,
(Roses that must be wooed,—nor may be won
Save by the prince of lovers, the warm sun),
Not the fair lily, nor the violet shy,
Whose heart's love lurks deep in her still blue eye,
Nor any flower, the loveliest and the best,
Can image to you half the charm compressed
In those dear eyes, those lips,—nay, every part
That made that sum of witcheries—Elfinhart.

21

Her face was a dim dream of shadowy light,
Like misty moonbeams on the fields of night,
And in her voice sweet nature's sweetest tunes
Sang the glad song of twenty cloudless Junes.
Her raiment,—nay; go, reader, if you please,
To some sage Treatise on Antiquities,
Whence writers of historical romances
Cull old embroideries for their new-spun fancies;
I care not for the trivial, nor the fleeting.
Beneath her dress a woman's heart was beating
The rhythm of love's eternal eloquence,
And I confess to you, in confidence,
Though flowers have grown a thousand years above her,
Unseen, unknown, with all my soul I love her.

From these digressions upon love and glory,
'Tis time we were returning to our story.
I only meant, in a few words, to tell you
(For fear my heroine's conduct should repel you)
That if she jests, for instance, out of season,
Perhaps there is a good substantial reason.
Sir Gawayne, had he seen the stranger wink
And seen the lady blushing, you may think
Might have been spared a most unhappy lot.
Perhaps you're right;—but peradventure not.
I give you but a hint, for half the art
Of narrative is holding back a part,
And if without reserve I gave my best
In the first canto, who would read the rest?

But now Sir Gawayne, with a troubled eye,
Looked up, and saw his lady standing by.
Quoth he: "And if this conjurer unblest
Win no acceptance of his bitter jest,
How then in after days shall Arthur's court

Confront the calumny and foul report
Of idle tongues?" The wrath in Gawayne's eyes
Hashed for an instant; then in humbler wise
He spoke on: "Yet God grant I be not blind
Where honor lights the way; for to my mind
True honor bids us shun the devil's den,
To fight God's battles in the world of men.
Who takes this challenge up, I doubt will rue it."
Quoth Elfinhart: "I'ld like to see you do it!"
She laughed a gay laugh, but by hard constraint:
Then turned and hid her face, all pale and faint,
As one might be who stabs and turns the knife
In the warm heart of one more dear than life.
She turned and Gawayne saw not; but he heard,
And felt his heart-strings tighten at her word.
"Nay, lady, if you wish it I will try;
Be your least wish my will, although I die!
Yet one thing, if I may, I fain would ask,
Before I make the venture;—if this task
Prove fateful as it threatens,—do you care?"
"Perhaps," said Elfinhart, "you do not dare!"
Lightly she laughed, and scoffing tossed her head,
Yet spoke as one who knew not what she said,
With random words, and with quick-taken breath;
Then turned again, ere that same look of death
Should steal upon her and betray her heart
Despite all stratagems of woman's art.
And Gawayne heard but saw not; and the night
Descended on him, and his face grew white
With grief and passion. When all else is lost,
The brave man gives life too, nor counts the cost.
"I dreamt," he murmured to himself, "and dreaming
I took for truth what was but sweetest seeming.
My waking eyes find naught in life to keep;
I take the venture, and so back—to sleep."

By this, the stranger had at last become
Tired of long waiting, and of sitting dumb
Upon his charger; so with greenest leer
He vented his impatience in a sneer.
"Is this," he said, "the glorious Table Round,
And is its glory naught but empty sound?
Braggarts! I put your bluster to the test,
And find you quail before a merry jest!"
Then the great king himself stood up in ire,
With clenched hand raised, and eyes that gleamed dark fire,
And fronting the Green Knight he cried: "Forbear!
For by my sword Excalibur I swear,

"Whate'er thou be, thou shalt not carry hence
Unscathed the memory of thine insolence.
Such jests as thine please not; yet even so
I take thine axe; kneel thou, and take my blow."

Across the Green Knight's features there was seen
To pass a fleeting shade of deeper green,
Whether of disappointment or resentment
None knew; but straight a smile of bright contentment
Followed, as through the throng of dazed beholders
He saw Sir Gawayne thrust his sturdy shoulders.
The stranger winked at Elfinhart once more,
Well pleased, and Gawayne knelt down on the floor.
"A boon," he cried, "a boon, my lord and king!
If ever yet in any little thing
These hands have served thee, hear my last request:
Let *me* adventure this mad monster's jest!"
King Arthur shook his head in dumb denial,
Loth to withdraw his own hand from the trial,
And leave the vengeance that himself had vowed;
But all the people called to him aloud,

"Sir Gawayne! let Sir Gawayne strike the blow!"
And Guinevere, the queen, besought him low
To leave this venture to the lesser man.
He yielded, and the merry jest began.

The visitor, dismounting, made a bow
To Arthur, then to all the court. "And now,"
Said he to Gawayne, "wheresoe'er you choose
To strike your blow, strike on; I'll not refuse;
Head, shoulders, chest, or waist, I little reck;
Where shall it be?" Quoth Gawayne, "In the neck!"

So Gawayne took the axe. The stranger knelt
Before him on the hearth and loosed his belt,
And threw back his green cassock and his hood,
To give his foe the fairest mark he could.
Then thus to Gawayne: "Ready! But remember
To come the twenty-fifth of next December,
And take from me the self-same stroke again!"
"And where," asked Gawayne, "may I find you then?"
"We'll speak of that, please, when you've struck your blow;
For if I can't speak, then you need not go!"
He chuckled softly to himself; then turned
And waited for the blow, all unconcerned.

Not so the knights and ladies of the court;
They pushed and craned their necks to see the sport;
Not from the lust of blood, for few expected
To see blood shed, or the Green Knight dissected,
But knowing that some marvel was in store
Unparalleled in all Arthurian lore,
And fairly filled with wide-eyed wonderment.
But Lady Elfinhart stayed not. She went
Into the alcove where we saw her first

And laid her sweet face in her arms, and burst
Into—but none could tell, unless by peeping,
Whether she shook with laughter or with weeping.

And Gawayne rubbed his arms, his chest he beat,
Then grasped the battle-axe and braced his feet,
And swung the ponderous weapon high in air,
And brought it down like lightning, fair and square
Upon the stranger's neck. The axe flashed through,
Cutting the Green Knight cleanly right in two,
And split the hard stone floor like kindling wood.
The head dropped off; out gushed the thick, hot blood
Like—I can't find the simile I want,
But let us say a flood of *crême de menthe*!
And then the warriors standing round about
Sent up from fifty throats a mighty shout,
As when o'er blood-sprent fields the long cheers roll
Cacophonous, for him who kicks a goal.

"O Gawayne! Well done, Gawayne!" they all cried;
But straight the tumult and the shouting died,
And deadly pallor overspread each face,
For the knight's body stood up in its place
And stepping nimbly forward seized the head
That lay still on the hearth-stone, seeming dead;
Then vaulted lightly, with a careless air,
Back to the saddle of his grass-green mare.
He held the head up, and behold! it spoke.
"My best congratulations on that stroke,
Sir Gawayne; it was delicately done!
Our merry little jest is well begun,
But look you fail me not this day next year!
At the Green Chapel by the Murmuring Mere
I will await you when the sun sinks low,
And pay you back full measure, blow for blow!"

He wheeled about, the doors flew wide once more,
The mare's hoofs struck green sparkles from the floor,
And with a whirring flash of emerald light
Both horse and rider vanished in the night.

Then all the lords and ladies rubbed their eyes
And slowly roused themselves from dumb surprise.
The great hall echoed once more with the clatter
Of laughing men's and frightened women's chatter;
But Gawayne, with the axe in hand, stood still,
Heedless of what was passing, with no will
For life or death, for all that made life dear
Was fled like summer when the leaves fall sere.
And Arthur spoke, misreading Gawayne's thought:
"Heaven send we have not all too dearly bought
Our evening's pastime, Gawayne. You have done
As fits a fearless knight, and nobly won
Our thanks in equal measure with our praise.
Be both remembered in the after days!"

So spoke the king, and, to confirm his word,
From far away in the deep night was heard
Once more the fairy horn-call, clear and shrill;
It died upon the wind, and all was still.
The hour was late. King Arthur, rising, said
Good-night to all his court, and went to bed.

CANTO II

ELFINHART

In Canto I. I followed the old rule
We learned from Horace when we went to school,
And took a headlong plunge *in medias res*,
As Maro did, and blind Mæonides;
And now, still following the ancient mode,
I come to the time-honored "episode,"
Retrace my way some twenty years or more,
And tell you what I should have told before.
It seems an awkward method, but it's art;—
Besides, it brings us back to Elfinhart.

In those dark days before King Arthur came,
When Britain was laid waste with sword and flame,
When cut-throats lurked behind the blossoming thorn,
And young maids cursed the day when they were born,
A lady, widowed in one hideous night,
Fled over heath and hill, and in her flight
Came to the magic willow-woods that stand
Beside the Murmuring Mere, in Fairyland;
And there, untimely, by the forest-side,
Clasping her infant in her arms, she died.
Yet not all friendless,—for such mortal throes
Pass not unpitied, though no mortal knows;—

The spirits that infest the clearer air
Looked down upon the innocent lady there,
While troops of fairies smoothed her mossy bed
And with sweet balsam pillowed her fair head.
Her dim eyes could not see them, but she guessed
Whose gentle ministrations thus had blessed
Her travail; and when pitying fairies laid
Upon her heart the child,—a blue-eyed maid,—
Ere yet her troubled spirit might depart,
With one last word she named her "Elfinhart."

So with new-quickened love the fairy elves
Took the forlorn child-maiden to themselves
And reared her in the wildwood, where no jar
Of alien discord, echoing from afar,
Broke the sweet forest murmur, long years round.
Her ears, attuned to every woodland sound,
Translated to her soul the great world's voice,
And the world-spirit made her heart rejoice.
And love was hers,—perennial, intense,—
The love that wells from joy and innocence
And sanctifies the cloistered heart of youth,—
The love of love, of beauty, and of truth.

So Elfinhart grew up. Each passing year
Of forest life beside the Murmuring Mere
Enriched tenfold the natural dower of grace
That shone from the pure spirit in her face.
I cannot tell why each revolving season
Enhanced her beauty thus. Some say the reason
Was in the stars; *I* think those luminaries
Had less to do with it than had the fairies!
The more they found of grace in her, the more
Their silent influence added to her store;

30

For they were always with her; they and she
Still bore each other loving company.

And yet one further virtue,—not the least
Of those that make life lovable,—increased
In Elfinhart's sweet nature from her birth
By fairy tutelage; and that was mirth.
For fairy natures are compounded all
Of whimsies and of freaks fantastical,
And what the best of fairies loves the best
(Except pure kindness) is an artless jest.
And so wise men have argued, on the whole,
That the misguided creatures have no soul;
But as for me, if the bright fairy elf
Has none, I'll get along without, myself!
These fairies laughed and danced and sang sweet songs,
And did all else that to their craft belongs,—
All tricks and pranks of whole-souled jollity
That make life merry 'neath the greenwood tree.
The youngest of them childishly beguiled
The time when Elfinhart was still a child;
They pinched her fingers, and they pulled her ears,
Or sometimes, when her blue eyes dreamed of tears,
Half smothered her with showers of four-leafed clover,—
Then fled for refuge to some sweet-fern cover;
But she pursued them through their tangled lair
And caught them, and put fire-flies in their hair;
And then they all joined hands, and round and round
They danced a morris on the moonlit ground.

The years went by, and Elfinhart outgrew
The madcap antics of the younger crew,
(For fairies age but slowly: don't forget
That at two hundred they are children yet!)

But still she frolicked with them, though scarce *of* them,
And learned each year more tenderly to love them.
But most of all she loved with all her heart
On quiet summer nights to walk apart
And hold close converse with the fairies' queen,—
A radiant maiden princess who had seen
Some twenty centuries of revolving suns
Pass over Fairyland,—all golden ones!
Sometimes they sat still in the mild moon's light,
Where chestnut blooms made sweet the breath of night,
And talked of the great world beyond the wood,—
Of death, or sin, or sorrow, understood
Of neither,—till the twinkling stars were gone,
And bustling Chanticleer proclaimed the dawn.
And Elfinhart grew wise in fairy learning;
But by degrees a half unconscious yearning
For humankind stirred in her gentle heart,
And woke a deep desire to bear her part
Of love and sorrow in the larger life
As sister, helper,—nay, perhaps as wife;—
For such vague instincts, after all, are human,
And Elfinhart herself was but a woman.
And yet, for all this new desire, I doubt
If Elfinhart would e'er have spoken out,
And told the fairies of her wish to leave them,
(A wish her conscious heart well knew would grieve them),
If in the ripening of her silent thought
A still voice had not whispered that she ought
To leave that world of love and mirth and beauty,
To share man's burden in this world of duty.
(There's anticlimax for you! Most provoking,
Just when you thought that I was only joking,
Or idly fingering the poet's laurel,
To find my story threatens to be moral!
But as for morals, though in verse we scout them,

In life we somehow can't get on without them;
So if I don't insert a moral distich
Once in a while, I can't be realistic;—
And in this tale, I solemnly aver,
My one wish is to tell things as they were!
But not *all* things; time flies, and art is long,
And I must hurry onward with my song.)
How Elfinhart at last told what she wanted,
And what the fairies said, please take for granted.
She prayed, they yielded; Elfinhart full loth
To leave, as they to let her go, but both
Agreeing that this bitter thing must be;
For they were fairies, and a mortal she.
But ere they yielded, they made imposition
Of what then seemed to her a light condition.
'Twas done in kindness, be it understood,
With fairy foresight for the maiden's good.
The elf-queen spoke for all: "Dear Elfinhart,
We bind you to one promise ere we part.
We fear naught from men's malice; hate and wrath
And every evil thing will shun your path,
And sunshine will go with you when you move;
The only danger that we dread is love.
If in the after days, when suitors woo you,
Your heart makes choice of one, as dearest to you,
Before you put your hand in his and own
The sacred trust reserved for him alone,
Let us make trial of him, and approve
His virtue, and his manhood, and his love.
Send him to us; and if he bears the test,
And if we find him worthy to be blest
With love like yours, be sure we will befriend him;
And may a life-long happiness attend him!
But if he prove a traitor, or faint-hearted,
Or if his love and he are lightly parted,

In the deep willow-woods he shall remain,
And never look upon your face again!"
The maiden, fancy-free, was well content,
And with light laughter gave her full consent;
For when maids think of love (as maidens do)
It seems a far-off thing; and well she knew
Her lover, if she loved, would be both brave and true!
Not long thereafter came an errant band
Riding along the edge of Fairyland,—
Stout men-at-arms, without reproach or spot,
And in the lead the bold Sir Launcelot.
He, riding on ahead, silent, alone,
Was stopped by a beseeching ancient crone
Who hobbled to his side, as if in pain,
And clutched with palsied fingers at his rein.
And there behind her, from the leafage green,
The sweetest eyes his eyes had ever seen
Were gazing at him with wide wonderment,
Nor bold nor fearful; innocence unshent
Shone from their blue depths, and old dreams awoke
In Launcelot's breast, while thus the beldame spoke:
"A boon, a boon, Sir Launcelot of the Lake!
I Pray you of your courtesy to take
This damsel to the King. Her enemies
Have spoiled her of her birthright, and she flees
An innocent outcast from her wasted lands,
To lay her life and fortune in his hands."
She spoke, and vanished in the woodland shade.

Then Launcelot, leaning over helped the maid
To mount behind and at an easy trot
They and the troop rode on to Camelot.
He asked no questions for some fairy spell
Made light his heart, and told him all was well;
And as these two rode through the land together,

By dappled greenwood shade and sunlit heather,
Her soft voice in his ears, the innocent charm
Of her light, steady touch upon his arm,
Wrought magic in his soul. That day, I ween,
Sir Launcelot well-nigh forgot his queen.
And Elfinhart (you knew those eyes were hers!)
Laughed with the silvery jingle of his spurs,
And from her heart the new world's rapture drove
All thought of Fairyland—excepting love.

And so to high-towered Camelot they came,
The golden city,—now a shadowy name;
For over heath-clad hills the wild-winds blow
Where Arthur's halls, a thousand years ago
Bright with all far-fetched gems of curious art,
Shone brighter with the eyes of Elfinhart.
She came to Camelot; the king receives her;
And there for five glad years my story leaves her.
Five glad years, and this "episode" is done,
And we are back again at Canto I.
I write of merry jest and greenwood shade,
But tales of chivalry are not my trade;
So if you wish to read that five years' story
Of lady-love, romance, and martial glory,—
The mighty feats of arms that Gawayne did,—
The ever ripening love that Gawayne hid
Five long years in his breast, biding his time,—
Go seek it in some abler poet's rime.
My tale begins with the young knight's brave soul
All Elfinhart's. She thinks herself heart-whole.

But at that Christmas feast, in Arthur's hall,
With night's soft mantle folded over all,
The magic influence of the evening tide
Stole on their two hearts beating side by side.

35

And Gawayne talked of troubles long ago,
When each man's neighbor was his dearest foe,
And of the trials he himself had passed,
And the high purpose that from first to last
Had been his stay and spur, he scarce knew how,
Since on Excalibur he took the vow.
He told of his own hopes for future days,
And how he wrought and fought not for men's praise,
(Though like all good men Gawayne held that dear),
Yet trusting, when men laid him on his bier,
They might remember, as they gathered round it,
"He left this good world better than he found it."
He talked as true men seldom talk, unless
Swayed utterly by some pure passion's stress,
And ever gently, though with heart on fire,
Still hovered nearer to his soul's desire.
And Elfinhart in gravest silence listened,
But her sweet heart beat high, her blue eyes glistened;
For as he bared his soul to her she dreamed
A day-dream strange and new, wherein it seemed
That in that soul's clear depth she saw her own,
And his most secret thought (till then unknown)
Seemed hers eternally. He spoke of death,
And then her heart shrank, and she drew deep breath.
Suddenly, ere she understood at all
What new life dawned before her, came the call
Of fairy horns; and so the Green Knight burst
Upon the scene, as told in Canto First.

One jarring note, the tuneful chords among,
May make mad discord of the sweetest song.
E'en so with dissonant clamor through the breast
Of Gawayne rang the Green Knight's merry jest;
But what wild meaning must it not impart
To the vague fears of gentle Elfinhart?

For she had heard in the first trumpet-blast
A signal to her from the far-gone past;
And now, of all the strange things that had been,
Her half forgotten compact with the queen
Flushed through her memory, and a swift thought came
Like sudden fear, a thought without a name,
An unvoiced question and a blind alarm;
And in sheer helplessness she reached an arm
Toward Gawayne scarcely knowing what she would;
Her eyes beheld him, and she understood.
And is it Gawayne? He? Yes, Elfinhart,
The hour has come, and you must play your part.

* * * * *

So now it's all explained; and I intend
To go straight onward to the story's end.
Sir Gawayne had cut off the Green Knight's head,
And Arthur and his court had gone to bed;
In the great hall the dying embers shone
With a faint ghostly gleam, and there, alone,
While all the rest of Camelot was sleeping,
In the dark alcove Elfinhart lay weeping.
But as she lay there, all about her head
There fell a checkered beam of moonlight, shed
Through the barred casement; and she faintly stirred,
For in her troubled soul it seemed she heard
Vague music from some region far away!
She raised her head and, turning where she lay,
Saw in the silver moonlight the serene
And tranquil beauty of the fairy queen!

"We sent before you called us, Elfinhart,
For love lent keener magic to our art,
And warned us of the thoughts that in your breast

Awoke new rapture, trembling unconfessed."
And Elfinhart moved closer to her knees
And hid her face in the white draperies
That veiled the fairy form, till, nestling there,
Her heart recovered from that blank despair,
And whispered her that whatsoe'er befell
Love ruled the world, and all would yet be well.
And the good fairy stroked the maiden's head
And kissed her tear-starred eyes, and smiling said:
"Fie on you women's hearts! Consistency
Hides her shamed head where mortal women be!
True love breeds faith and trust, it makes hearts strong;
The heart's anointed king can do no wrong!
And yet you weep as if you feared to prove him;—
Upon my word, I don't believe you love him!"
And Elfinhart replied: "Laugh if you will,
My queen, but let me be a woman still.
You fairies love where love is wise and just;
We mortal women love because we must:
And if I feared to prove him, I confess
I fear I still must love him none the less."
She paused, for once again her eyes grew dim:
"Think you I love his virtues? I love him!
But yet you judged me wrongly, for believe me,
(And then laugh once again, and so forgive me),
If at the first I feared what you might do,
My doubts were not of Gawayne, but of you!"
And so both laughed, and for a little space
Folded each other in a glad embrace;
(For fairies, bathed the whole year round in bliss,
May yet be gladdened by a fair maid's kiss);
And Elfinhart spoke on: "Do what you will,
I trust you with my all, and fear no ill.
But oh, my friend, to wait the long, long year,—
To keep my heart in silence, not to hear

The words my whole soul hungers for, nor say
One syllable to brighten his dark day!
Must it be so, my queen? And how shall I
School eyes and lips to act this year-long lie?
From the dear teacher-guardian of my youth
The only ways I learned were ways of truth!
I tried my skill this night, and learned to know
That there are deeps below the deeps of woe;
Hearts may be bruised and broken, yet still live;—
The wounds that kill us are the wounds we give!"

And so these two talked on, until the night
Began to shiver with the gray dawn's light,
And in the deep-dyed casement they might see
New life flush through old dreams of chivalry.
And then they parted. What the queen had said
I know not, but the lady, comforted,
Bade farewell with calm voice and tranquil eyes,
And saw with new-born strength the new sun rise.
Perhaps in Fairyland there chanced to be
For them that grieve some sovereign alchemy
To turn the worst to best, and the good queen
Applied this soothing balm. Such things have been;
But yet I doubt if any fairy art
Was needed in the case of Elfinhart;
The medicine that charmed away her dole
Nature had planted in her own sweet soul.
Of all sure things, this thing I'm surest of,—
That the best cure for love's own ills is love.

CANTO III

GAWAYNE

O Muse!—But no: heaven knows I need a muse;
But which of all the nine, pray, should I choose?
Thalia, Clio, and Melpomene,
I love them all, but none, alas, loves me;
For if you want a muse to take your part
You must be solely hers with all your heart;
And I have mingled since my earliest youth
My smiles and tears, my fictions and my truth;
Nay, in this very tale, scarce yet half done,
I've courted all the nine, and so won none!
Not for me, therefore, the Parnassian lyre,
Or winged war-horse shod with heavenly fire;
Harsh numbers flow from throats whose thirst has been
A whole life long unslaked of Hippocrene;
But I will e'en go on as best I can
And let the story end as it began,—
A plain, straightforward man's unvarnished word,
Part sad, part sweet,—and part of it absurd.

A year passed by, as years are wont to do,
Winter and spring, summer and autumn too,
Till mid-December's flaw-blown flakes of snow
Warned Gawayne that the time was come to go

To the Green Chapel by the Murmuring Mere,
And take again the blow he gave last year.
In the great court his charger stamped the ground,
While knights and weeping ladies thronged around
To arm him (as the custom was of yore)
And bid him sad farewell for evermore.
One face alone in all that bustling throng
Our hero's eyes sought eagerly, and long
Sought vainly; for the lady Elfinhart,
Debating with herself, stood yet apart;
But as Sir Gawayne gathered up his reins
And bade the draw-bridge warden loose the chains,
Suddenly Elfinhart stood by his side,
Her fair face flushed with love, and joy, and pride.
She plucked a sprig of holly from her gown
And looked up, questioning; and he leaned down,
And so she placed it in his helm. No word
Might Gawayne's lips then utter, but he heard
The voice that was his music, and could feel
The touch of gentle fingers through the steel.
"Wear this, Sir Gawayne, for a loyal friend
Whose hopes and prayers go with you to the end."
And, staying not for answer, she withdrew,
And in the throng was lost to Gawayne's view.
He roused himself, and waving high his hand,
Struck spur, and so rode off toward Fairyland.

Long time he traveled by an unknown way,
Unhoused at night, companionless by day.
The cold sleet stung him through his shirt of mail,
But, underneath, his stout heart would not fail,
But beat full measure through the fiercest storm,
And kept his head clear and his brave soul warm.
No need to tell the perils that he passed;
He conquered all, and came unscathed at last

To where a high-embattled castle stood
Deep in the heart of a dense willow-wood.
And Gawayne called aloud, and to the gate
A smiling porter came, who opened straight,
And bade him enter in and take his rest;
And Gawayne entered, and the people pressed
About him with fair speeches; and he laid
His armor off, and gave it them, and prayed
That they would take his message to their lord,—
Prayer for friendly shelter, bed and board.
He told them whence he was, his birth and name;
And the bold baron of the castle came,
A mighty man, huge-limbed, with flashing eyes,
And welcomed him with old-time courtesies;
For manners, in those days, were held of worth,
And gentle breeding went with gentle birth.
He heartily was glad his guest had come,
And made Sir Gawayne feel himself at home;
And as they walked in, side by side, each knew
The other for an honest man and true.

That night our hero and the baron ate
A sumptuous dinner in the hall of state,
And all the household, ranged along the board,
Made good cheer with Sir Gawayne and their lord,
And passed the brimming bowl right merrily
With friendly banter and quick repartee.
And Gawayne asked if they had chanced to hear
Of a Green Chapel by a Murmuring Mere,
And straightway all grew grave. Within his breast
Sir Gawayne felt a tremor of unrest,
But told his story with a gay outside,
And asked for some good man to be his guide
To find his foe. "I promise him," said he,
"No golden guerdon;—his reward shall be

The consciousness that unto him 't was given
To show a parting soul the way to heaven!"

Up jumped his host. "My friend, I like your attitude,
And know no surer way to win heaven's gratitude
Than sending thither just such men as you;
I'll be your guide. But since you are not due
At the Green Chapel till three nights from now,
And since the way is short, I'll tell you how
The interim may be disposed of best:—
In short, let me propose a merry jest!"
At this Sir Gawayne gave a sudden start,
For some old memory seemed to clutch his heart,
And in the baron's eyes he seemed to see
A twinkling gleam of green benignity
Not wholly strange; but like a flash 't was gone.
Gawayne sank back, and his good host went on:
"Two days you sojourn here, and while I take
My daily hunting in the wood, you make
My house and castle yours; and then, each night,
We'll meet together here at candle-light,
And all my winnings in the wood, and all
That comes to you at home, whate'er befall,
We'll give each other in exchange; in fine,
My fortune shall be yours, and yours be mine."
To Gawayne this seemed generous indeed.
And with most cordial laughter he agreed.
They clasped hands o'er the bargain with good zest,
And then all said good-night, and went to rest.

Next morning Gawayne was awakened early
From a deep slumber by the hurly-burly
Of footman, horseman, seneschal, and groom,
Bustling beneath the windows of his room.
He rose and looked out, just in time to see

The baron and a goodly company
Of huntsmen, armed with cross-bow, axe, and spear,
Ride through the castle gate and disappear.
And then, while Gawayne dressed, there came a knock
Upon his chamber door. He threw the lock,
And a boy page brought robes of ermine fur
And Tarsic silk,—black, white, and lavender,—
For his array, and with them a kind message,
Which the good knight received with no ill presage:
"Will brave Sir Gawayne spare an idle hour
For quiet converse in my lady's bower?"
The boy led on, and Gawayne followed him
Through crooked corridors and archways dim,
Along low galleries echoing from afar,
And down a winding stair; then "Here we are!"
The page cried cheerily, and paused before
The massive carvings of an antique door.
This he swung open; and the knight passed through
Into a garden, fresh with summer dew!
A lady's bower in Fairyland! What pen
Could make that strange enchantment live again?
Not he who drew Acrasia's Bower of Bliss
And Phædria's happy isle could picture this.
That sweet-souled Puritan discerned too well
The serpent's coil behind the witch's spell;
And he who saw—when the dark veil was torn—
The rose of Paradise without the thorn,
(Sublimest prophet, whose immortal verse
Lent mightier thunders to the primal curse),
Even he too sternly, in the soul's defense,
Repressed the still importunate cries of sense.
Bid me not, therefore, task my feebler pen
With dreams beyond the limits of their ken;
The phantom conjurings of the magic hour
That Gawayne passed in that enchanted bower

Must be from mortal eyes forever hid.
But yet some part of what he felt and did
These lines must needs disclose. As he stood there,
Breathing soft odors from the mellow air,
All hopes, all aims of noble knighthood seemed
Like the dim yesterdays of one who dreamed,
In starless caves of memory sunken deep,
And, like lost music, folded in strange sleep.

"How long, O mortal man, wilt thou give heed
To the world's phantom voices? The hours speed,
And fame and fortune yield to moth and rust,
And good and evil crumble into dust.
Even now the sands are running in the glass;
Set not your heart upon vain things that pass;
Ambitions, honors, toils, are but the snare
Where lurks for aye the blind old world's despair.
Nay, quiet the bootless striving in your breast
And let your tired heart here at last find rest.
In vain have joy, love, beauty, struck deep root
In your heart's heart, unless you pluck the fruit;
Then put away the cheating soul's pretense,
Heap high the press, fill full the cup of sense;
Shatter the idols of blind yesterday,
And let love, joy, and beauty reign alway!"

Such thoughts as these, confused and unexpressed,
Flooded the silence in Sir Gawayne's breast.
Meanwhile a brasier filled the scented air
With wreaths of magic mist, and he was ware
That the mist drew together like a shroud;
And then the veil was rent, and in the cloud
Stood one who seemed, in features, form, and dress,
The perfect image of all loveliness.

The wonders of that vision none could tell
Save one whose heart had felt the mystic spell.
Once and once only, in the golden days
When youth made melody for love's sweet lays,
In two dark eyes (yet oh, how bright, how bright!)
I saw the wakening rapture of love's light,
And, in the hush of that still dawning, heard
From two sweet trembling lips love's whispered word.
The twilight deepens when the sun has set;
In memory golden glories linger yet;
But these avail not. Though my soul lay bare,
With all those memories sanctuaried there,
That spell was human. But the unseen power
That wove the witchery of this fairy bower,
In Gawayne's heart such subtle magic wrought
That past and future were well-nigh forgot,
And all that earth holds else, or heaven above,
Seemed naught worth keeping, save this dream of love.

And now, as the strange cloud of incense broke,
The vision, if it were a vision, spoke,—
If it were speech that filled the quivering air
With low harmonious music. Let none dare
In the rude jargons of this world to fashion
That sweet, wild anthem of unearthly passion.
Could I from the broad-billowing ocean borrow
Of Tristan's love and of Isolde's sorrow,
The flood of those world-darkening surges, wrought
With thoughts that lie beyond the reach of thought,
Might bring me succor where weak words must fail.
But Gawayne saw and heard, and passion-pale
Shrank back, and made a darkness of his face;
(As though the unplumbed deeps of starless space
Could quench those lustrous eyes, or close his ears
To the eternal music of love's spheres!)

47

But the voice changed, and Gawayne, listening there,
Heard now a heart's low cry of wild despair.
He turned again, and lo! the vision knelt
And drew a jeweled poniard from her belt,
To arm herself against her own dear life;
But as she bared her white breast to the knife
He started quickly forward, and he grasped
The hand that held the hilt; and then she clasped
Her soft arms round his neck, and as their lips
Met in the shadowing fold of love's eclipse,
All earth, all heaven, all knightly hopes of grace,
Died in the darkness of one blind embrace.

Died? Nay; for Gawayne, ere the moment passed,
Broke from the arms that strove to bind him fast,
And turned away once more; and, as he pressed
A trembling hand against his throbbing breast,
His aimless fingers touched a treasured part
Of the green holly-branch of Elfinhart,
Laid in his breast when he put off his arms.
What perils now are left in fairy charms?
For poets fable when they call love blind;
Love's habitation is the purer mind,
Whence with his keen eyes he may penetrate
All mists and fogs that baser spells create.
Love? What is love? Not the wild feverish thrill,
When heart to heart the thronging pulses fill,
And lips that close in parching kisses find
No speech but those;—the best remains behind.
The tranquil spirit—the divine assurance
That this life's seemings have a high endurance—
Thoughts that allay this restless striving, calm
The passionate heart, and fill old wounds with balm;—
These are the choirs invisible that move
In white processionals up the aisles of love.

Such love was Gawayne's,—love that sanctifies
The heart's most secret altar; and his eyes
Their old true rhythm. And so the strife was o'er,
And all the perilous wiles of magic art
Were foiled by Gawayne—and by Elfinhart.

But time flies, and 't were tedious to delay
My song for all the trials of that day.
Light summer breezes, skurrying o'er the deep,
Ripple and foam and flash,—then sink to sleep;
But underneath, serene and changing never,
The mighty heart of ocean beats forever,
And his deep streams renew from pole to pole
The living world's indomitable soul.
Enough, then, of the spells that vexed the brain
Of Gawayne; love and knighthood made all vain.

And in the afternoon, when Gawayne learned
That his good host, the baron, had returned,
He met him in the hall at candle-light,
According to his promise of last night.
And then the baron motioned to a page,
And straightway six tall men, of lusty age
And mighty sinews, entered the great door,
Bearing the carcass of a huge wild boar,
In all its uncouth ugliness complete,
And dropped it quivering at our hero's feet.
"What do you say to that, Sir Gawayne?" cried
The baron, swelling with true sportsman's pride
"But come: your promise, now, of yester-eve;
'T is blesseder to give than to receive!
Though I'll be sworn you'll find it hard to pay
Full value for the winnings of this day."
"Not so," said Gawayne; "you will rest my debtor;
Your gift is good, but mine will be far better."

And then he strode with solemn steps along
The echoing hall, and through the listening throng,
And with the words, "My noble lord, take this!"
He gave the baron a resounding kiss.
The baron jumped up in ecstatic glee.
"Now by my great-great-grandsire's beard," quoth he,
"Better than all dead boars in Christendom
Is one sweet loving kiss!—Whence did it come?"
"Nay, there," Sir Gawayne said, "you step beyond
The terms we stipulated in our bond.
Take you my kiss in peace, as I your boar;
Be glad; give thanks;—and seek to know no more."
Loud laughter made the baron's eyes grow bright
And glitter with green sparkles of delight;
And then he chuckled: "Sir, I'm proud of you;
I drink your best of health; *I think you'll do!"*

And now the board was laid and dressed, and all
Sat down to dinner at the baron's call;
And Gawayne looked along the room askance,
Seeking the lady; and he caught one glance
Of laughing eyes—then looked away in haste,
But turned again, and wondered why his taste
Had erred so strangely, for the lady seemed
Not fairer now than others. Had he dreamed?
He rubbed his eyes and pondered,—though in sooth
Without one glimmering presage of the truth,—
Till all passed lightly from his puzzled mind,
Leaving contentment and good cheer behind.
So all the company feasted well, and sped
The flying hours, till it was time for bed.

One whole day longer must our hero rest
Within doors, to fulfill the merry jest.
So when, next morning, Gawayne once more heard

The hunt's-up in the court, he never stirred,
But let the merry horsemen ride away
While he slept soundly well into the day.
Later he rose, and strolled from room to room,
Through vaulted twilights of ancestral gloom,
Until, descending a long stair, he found
The dim-lit castle crypt, deep under ground,
Where sculptured effigies forever kept
Their long last marble silence as they slept,
And iron sentinels, on bended knees,
Held eyeless vigil in old panoplies.

Sir Gawayne, wandering on in aimless mood,
Pondered the tomb-stone legends, quaint and rude,
Wherein the pensive dreamer might divine
A tragic history in every line;
For so does fate, with bitterest irony,
Epitomize fame's immortality,
Perpetuating for all after days
Mute lamentations and unnoted praise.
And Gawayne, reading here and there the story
Of fame obscure and unremembered glory,
Found on a tablet these words: "Where he lies,
The gray wave breaks and the wild sea-mew flies:
If any be that loved him, seek not here,
But in the lone hills by the Murmuring Mere."
A nameless cenotaph!—perhaps of one
Like Gawayne's self deluded and undone
By the green stranger; and the legend brought
A tide of passion flooding Gawayne's thought;
A flood-tide, not of fear,—for Gawayne's breast
Shrank never at the perilous behest
Of noble knighthood,—but the love of life,
Compassion, and soul-sickness of the strife.
"If any be that loved him!" Oh, to die

Far from green-swarded Camelot, and lie
Among these bleak and barren hills alone,
His end unwept for and his grave unknown,—
Never again to see the glad sunrise
That brightened all his world in those dear eyes!

Half suffocating in the charneled air
Of that low vault, he staggered up the stair,
Out of the dim-lit halls of silent death
Into the living light, and drew quick breath
Where, through a casement-arch of ivied stone,
Bright from the clear blue sky the warm sun shone.
The whole of life's glad rapture thrilled his heart;
Till a quick step behind him made him start,
And there, deep-veiled, in muffling cloak and hood,
Once more the lady of the castle stood.

Low-voiced she spoke, as if with studied care
Weighing the syllables of her parting prayer.
"Sir Gawayne—nay, I pray you, turn not yet,
But hear me;—though my heart may not forget
That once, for one sweet moment, you were kind,
I come not to recall that to your mind;—
Between us two be love's words aye unspoken!
Yet ere you go, I pray you, leave some token
That in the long, long years may comfort me
For the dear face I nevermore shall see."
"Nay, lady," said the knight, "I have no gifts
To give you. Errant knighthood ever drifts
From shore to shore, by wandering breezes blown,
With naught save its good name to call its own.
In friendship, then, I pray you keep for me
My name untarnished in your memory."
"Ah, sir," she said, "my memory bears that name
Burnt in with characters of living flame.

But though you give me naught, I pray you take
This girdle from me;—wear it for my sake;
Nay, but refuse me not; you little know
Its magic power. I had it long ago
From Fairyland; and its encircling charm
Keeps scathless him who wears it from all harm;
No evil thing can touch him. Gird it on,
If but to ease my heart when you are gone."

She held a plain green girdle in her hand,
In outward seeming just a narrow band
Of silk, with silver clasps; but in those days
The strangest things were wrought in simplest ways,
As Gawayne knew full well; and he could see
That all the lady said was verity.
He took the girdle, held it, fingered it,
Then clasped it round his waist to try the fit,
Irresolutely dallying with temptation,
Till conscience grew too weak for inclination;
For at the last he threw one wandering glance
Out at the casement, and the merry dance
Of sparkling sunbeams on the fields of snow
Wrought havoc in his wavering heart; and so,
Repeating to himself one word: "Life, life!"
He took the token from the baron's wife.

That evening, when the baron and our knight
Met to exchange their gifts at candle-light,
The baron, looking graver than before,
Said: "Sir, my luck has left me; not a boar
Did we get wind of, all this blessed day.
I come with empty hands, only to pray
Your pardon. What good fortune do *you* bring?"
And Gawayne answered firmly: "Not a thing!"

CANTO IV

CONCLUSION

By noon the next day, Gawayne and his host
Rode side by side along the perilous coast
Of the gray Mere, from whose unquiet sleep
Reverberating murmurs of the deep
Startled the still December's listening air.
The baron, shuddering, pointed seaward. "There,"
He said, "year in, year out, these voices haunt
That fearful water; heaven knows what they want!
Men tell me—and I have no doubt it's true—
They are knights-errant whom the Green Knight slew!
Woe unto him, the over-bold, who dares
Adventure near that uncouth monster's snares!"
Quoth Gawayne: "How have *you* escaped the net?"
The baron answered: "I? We never met!
When I'm about, he seems to shun the place,
And where he is, I never show my face;
But if we did meet, 't would be safe to say
Not more than one of us would get away!"

And then the baron told tales by the score
About the Green Knight's quenchless thirst for gore,
And kept repeating that no magic charm
Was proof against the prowess of his arm;

At his first blow each vain defense must fall,
For he was arch-magician over all.
And as from tale to tale the baron ran,
Sir Gawayne, had he been another man,
Would certainly have felt his heart's blood curdle,
Despite his secret wearing of the girdle;
But when the baron finally suggested
Abandoning the venture, and protested
That the whole monstrous business was absurd,
Sir Gawayne simply said: "I gave my word."
And when the baron saw he would not bend,
He seemed to lose all patience. "Well, my friend,
I'll go no further with you. On your head
Shall be your own mad blood when you are dead.
Yonder your two roads fork; pause there, I pray,
And ponder well before you choose your way.
One takes the hills, one winds along the wave;
To Camelot this,—the other to your grave!
Choose the high road, Sir Gawayne; shun the danger!
Say you were misdirected by a stranger;—
I swear by all that's sacred, I'll not tell
One syllable to a soul:—and so farewell!"
He galloped off without another word,
And vanished where the road turned. Gawayne heard,
Long after he had disappeared, the sound
Of iron hoof-beats on the frozen ground,
Till all died into silence, save those drear
And hollow voices from the Murmuring Mere.

But Gawayne chose the lower road, and passed
Along the desolate shore. The die was cast.
The western skies, as the red sun sank low,
Cast purple shades across the drifted snow,
And Gawayne knew that the dread hour was come
For the fulfillment of his martyrdom.

And now, from just beyond a jutting hill,
Came hideous sounds, as of a giant mill
That hisses, roars, and sputters, clicks and clacks;—
It was the Green Knight sharpening his axe!
And Gawayne, coming past the corner, found him,
With ghastly mouldering skulls and bones strewn round him,
In joyous fury urging the keen steel
Against the surface of his grinding wheel.
The place was a wild hollow, circled round
With barren hills, and on the bottom ground
Stood the Green Chapel, moss-grown, solitary;—
In sooth, it seemed the devil's mortuary!
The Green Knight's back was turned, and he stirred not
Till Gawayne hailed him sharply; then he shot
One glance—as when, o'erhead, a living wire
Startles the night with flashes of green fire;—
Then hurried forward, bland as bland could be,
And greeted Gawayne with green courtesy.
"Dear sir, I ask a thousand pardons; pray
Forgive me. You are punctual to the day;
That's good! Of course I knew you would not fail.
How do you do? You look a trifle pale;
I trust, with all my heart, you are not ill?
Just the cold air? It does blow rather chill!
What can I do to cheer you? Let me see;—
Suppose I brew a cup of hot green tea?
You'ld rather not? You're pressed for time? Of course,
I understand; then just get off your horse,
And I'll do all I can to expedite
Our little business for you. There, that's right;
And now your helmet? Thanks; and if you please
Perhaps you'll kindly kneel down on your knees,
As I did when I came to Camelot; So!
Are you all ready? Will you bide the blow?"
And Gawayne said "I will," in such soft notes

As happy bridegrooms utter, when their throats
Are paralyzed with blest anticipation;—
(What Gawayne looked for was decapitation!)
And then the Green Knight swung his axe in air
With a loud whirr; and Gawayne, kneeling there,
Shrank back an inch; and the green giant stayed
His threatening hand, and with a cold sneer said:
"You shrink, sir, from the axe; I can't hit true
Unless you hold still, as I did for you."
"Your pardon," Gawayne said, with bated breath;
"This time I swear to hold as still as death."
He did so, and the Green Knight swung again
His axe, and whirled it round his head, and then,
Pausing a second time, said: "Very good!
You're holding quite still now; I knew you would!"
Gawayne, in anger, said: "Jest, if you like,
After the blow; tarry no longer; strike!"
So once again the ponderous axe was raised;
But this time down it came, and lightly grazed
Sir Gawayne's neck. He felt the hot blood flow,
And saw red drops that sank deep in the snow,
And then he jumped up, faced his foe, and cried:
"Enough: you owed me one blow, though I died;
But be you man or beast or devil abhorred,
I yield no further; with my mortal sword
I do defy you; and if mortal man
May hope against" . . .
⠀⠀⠀⠀⠀⠀⠀⠀⠀⠀⠀But the Green Knight began
A low melodious laugh, like running brooks
Whose pebbly babble fills the shadowy nooks
Of green-aisled woodlands, when the winds are still.
"My friend, we bear each other no ill will.
When first I swung my axe, you showed some fear;
I owed you that much for your blow last year.
The second time I swung,—yet spared your life,—

That paid you for the kiss you gave my wife!"
"Your wife!" "My wife, Sir Gawayne; 't was my word;
And when I swung my weapon for the third
And last time, then I made the red blood spirt
For that green girdle underneath your shirt!
You played me false, my friend!"
                And Gawayne knelt
Once more, and casting off the magic belt,
In bitter broken words confessed his shame,
And begged the Green Knight to avenge the name
Of injured knighthood, and with one last blow
To end his guilty life. "Nay, nay, not so,"
The other softly said. "Be of good cheer;
Your fault was small, for all men hold life dear.
We tempted you, my friend, with all our might,
And proved you in good sooth a noble knight;
A veritable Joseph, sir, you are!"
Quoth Gawayne drily, "Thanks, Lord Potiphar!
But may I ask you why you played this part?"
The other said: "Ask Lady Elfinhart!"

He smiled, and from his smile a genial glow
Of green mid-summer seemed to overflow,
Filling with verdure all that barren place.
The warm red blood rushed to Sir Gawayne's face;
He caught his breath, and in his eager eyes
There shone a sudden flash of dark surmise,
And then he stood a long while pondering;
But in his breast his heart began to sing
The old, old music whose still echoes roll
Forever voiceless through the listening soul.
He said farewell to his good fairy friend
As in a dream, where real and unreal blend
In phantom unison, and with the light
Of love to lead him home, rode through the night,

59

Beside the tranquil murmurs of the Mere,
And through the silence of the passing year;
And earth and sea and starlit sky took part
In the still exaltation of his heart,
While all but love and wonder was forgot,
Until he came to high-towered Camelot.

To Camelot he came, and there he found
The good King Arthur and his Table Round
Awaiting his return in anxious doubt;
But ere he passed the gates a mighty shout
Rose from the watchmen on the outward wall
And bore the tidings to the inmost hall.
From every window flaunting flags were flung;
From the high battlements brass trumpets sung;
And great bells, chiming in the topmost tower,
Pealed salutation to the joyous hour,
As Gawayne, riding through the cullis-port,
Faced the glad throng that filled the palace court.

And with this tribute paid to knightly glory
It seems most fitting to conclude my story.
Entreat me not, dear reader, to impart
Further of Gawayne, or of Elfinhart.
Let your own fancy round the story out
Whatever way you please; I cannot doubt
The sequel; but when I, in silent thought,
Had brought Sir Gawayne back to her, and sought
With hand profane to lift the veil, behind
Whose secret shelter their two hearts enshrined
The mutual covenant of love's mystery,
That pure fane would not desecrated be.
But this alone I know: the power that wove
Through human lives the warp and woof of love
Wrought not in darkness, nor with hand unsure;—

His fabric must forevermore endure.
And hence I doubt not that these two were blest
As none may be, save they who have confessed
Allegiance to that mighty spirit's law,
And trod his holy ground with reverent awe.

Printed in Great Britain
by Amazon